# Lives in London
# Variety of Short Other Stories

## By

## Taseen Khan

Taseen Khan

Published in 2012

By Taseem Khan


The right of Taseem Khan to be identified as the author of this work has been asserted by him in accordance with the copyright, Designs and Patents act 1988

ISBN **978-0-9573901**.

Sponsored by: Euro Tandoori , Chilli Shaker, Tasneem Travel, Rowza and Brothers Ltd and Bangla Shur
Printed by: Russell Press
Edited by: Adam Harrison and Mike Coates

Taseen Khan

# Contents

Taseen Khan

I've read with great interest and enjoyment Taseen's stories and play scripts, written when he was ten. They show good insights to the community life in the local area, but coupled with creativity and imagination. Very glad to hear he is still writing, and working with "Scene and Heard". I wish him every success in the future.

***Cllr Peter Brayshaw for St Pancras and Somers Town ward***

'Taseen Khan has a keen eye and special ear for the beat of everyday life. His stories and plays are full of spirit and telling detail. A local talent to watch out for. Edith Neville should take pride in one of their star pupils.''

***Angela Mason CBE***
***Cabinet Member for Children***
***London Borough of Camden***
***Taseen Khan- a writer of high prospect......***

Taseen Khan

# Foreword

My name is Taseen Khan and I'm twelve years old at the moment and I decided to write this book. So read below as I tell you how my book was made.

It was around three thirty in the afternoon and it was raining as usual during what was meant to be the "summer holidays'. My mum was telling me to write a book.

What can I say, I mean, I was on the road to becoming a footballer then my dreams just got shattered like an ant getting squished without noticing. Then my journey started as a cricketer. It was all going good until my football career was getting back on the road.

Football or cricket?

By the way, did you know I actually wrote the book when I was ten, taking me two years to publish it? I blame my mum because she was busy with politics during the process of my book

Taseen Khan

producing. I mean that's why it took so long for this book to get published.

Go on, turn on to the next page as you will get wonders of brilliance and extraordinary intelligence and … okay maybe I'm exaggerating just a little?

Let me tell you more about me and my life:

I never meant to be a writer, it just wasn't my dream. I always wanted to be a footballer. I played for the David Beckham Academy in Greenwich, I then joined my first club, Somers Town Future, and after a bit I moved onto Pro Touch Soccer Academy. Overall I was a good player, but my communication skills were bad, but I sure had the game play. After I knew that my football career might not be working, I decided I needed a new path. So I decided to join my school cricket team then my mum told me I should join Regent's Park Cricket Club. Guess what I think I am really enjoying cricket and maybe I should be playing for England one day ... who knows, maybe I will.

Taseen Khan

By the way, did I tell you that I love reading books and my favorite book is Diary of a Wimpy kid, I must say that I have read all the books written the by the Author and he is one of my favorite author?

My mum kept on nagging me to finish off the story I started; she told me s he really enjoys reading my stories. That's when I saw my dad reading this book to my baby brother. This wasn't an ordinary book though. This was a book called 'Jibber Jabber Journeys' and this book had an extract of my story I wrote when I was in year 3 (7 years old). It was called 'The Soldier'. Here's the full story (yep, it's that short): 'On my way to school I saw a soldier. His eyes were green. I stole his car. He was mean and ugly and big like a spider. He was fat and he had a green tongue. His tongue was big and long. He chased me. It was cool. He said "You have to stop. If you don't I will tell the cats to eat you." I said "I am going to tell my dragon to eat you and you are going to be mad." This story was the story that decided to change my life and helped me give birth to this book that you are holding. Any ways, since this is my biography let's get started............. I've got

Taseen Khan

one brother, Takbeer Khan, and one sister, Rowza Khan. If you were wondering who the eldest is, go read this biography again. It says it on the top. No really, go read it from the top. I'm not joking. Okay, yeah, I am joking, I'm the eldest obviously. I'm writing the 'haha' now.

I went to Edith Neville Primary School – this is the best school. Hopefully my brother and sister will go there too. My two best friends went to Central Foundations Boys' School so I decided to follow them. Shall I tell you a bit about my secondary school journey……? It's long but, what can I say, the first day I was nervous and shy. I was really scared because I heard these stories of bullying and that in your first year. Well lucky me, I was fine and gradually got familiar with everyone. Now I have many friends in the school. This is the best school.

Now that's done let me just mention some names of people that have been a great help to me during my book process and throughout my life, the people who have practically inspired me. It's a long list so here we go:
I am proud to say how delightful I am to have

Taseen Khan

such a wonderful family, who had courage me to finish this book. Very special thanks to my dad Sajjad Khan, mum Cllr Samata Khatoon, and my grandma (Nani), Aymona Khatoon.

This is to all my buddies (cousin brothers) who encourage me to write this book Wamiq, Faiz ,Wafiq, Ibrahim and two of my special uncle Alamin and Al-maktum

A very special thanks to Marlene Lai and Cllr Jenny Headlam-Wells for their support and encouragement for me to write this book and they were the very first persons to read this book (2 years ago) their kind words has motivated me and has boosted my confidence to complete this book.

**Big thanks to Cllr Adam Harrison and Mike Coates for editing and proof reading my book.**

Thanks to my uncles who sponsored this book, Md Gazi, Soydur Rahman and Ahmed Hasan

**Businesses: Euro Tandoori , Chilli Shaker, Tasneem Travel, Rowza and Brothers Ltd and Bangla Shur** Thanks to John Carroll for taking my photos.

Taseen Khan

**I am incredibly honoured to get an endorsement of my book by our Local MP, Right Honourable MP Frank Dobson, Honourable MP Luciana Berger and The Leader of Camden Council Sarah Hayward and all the councilors local residents and everyone else, (you know who you are)... Thank you.**

Also thanks to Scene & Heard. Scene & Heard is a unique mentoring project that brings together the inner-city children of Somers Town, London, with volunteer theatre professionals to create original theatre. I love them!

By the way, I have decided to support the charity organization Scene and Heard.

Finally, before I go let me tell you about my next book, I have already started to write it, is called 'Choose your Path?'

Taseen Khan

"Janet and I have read Taseen Khan's short stories and plays. All the best fiction tells a good tale and Taseen does just that. His stories display a talent and sense of humour beyond his years. They pass the ultimate test – the stories are a good read and the little plays are great fun."

*Right Honourable MP Frank Dobson*
*Parliament Member for Holborn and*
*St Pancras*

I really enjoyed reading this collection of short stories and plays, particularly 'My life in London' which captures one family's Olympic experience. Taseen has a wonderful imagination which is infused by an acute observation of day to day life in North London. For someone so young it is a great achievement to have this collection published. I wish Taseen every success now and in the future.

*Luciana Berger*
*Labour and Co-operative Member of*
*Parliament for Liverpool Wavertree*
*Shadow Minister for Climate Change*

Taseen Khan

Taseen, it was a real charm to read your book. You have pulled me back to my young age as you are now. Exactly on your present age I have started my immature stage performance in drama, writing scripts, stories, poems (in Bengali) but never had a chance to publish but I didn't stop my hobby.

I never knew it could be a sleeping seed raising her arms to hug the world of literature, could be a raising sun swapping out of the cloud to brighten the sky.

Taseen I will be waiting to see you as a writer and many more books on the way. If I am not there the world will see you.

I wish your very good health and success in all aspect of your future.

*Uncle Nurul Islam Putul*
*Ex Mayor, London Borough of Camden.*

Taseen Khan

Anyways, just start reading the book. I mean it.

## The first story

## Me and the society

It was Sunday morning and I could smell the spices of a delicious curry spreading around the house with the air – it was my mum cooking. She always would wake up at eight in the morning then start cooking for seven people.

My life is pretty tough, you know I wake up around eight thirty (which I hate), then I have to step over four people to get out of my room. Can you imagine how hard it is? I mean a two-bedroom flat being shared by seven people! Pretty amazing I'd say.

As soon as I stepped out of the room, I could already see the queue for the bathroom. And guess who has been their since eight for half an hour and who is still in there? My sister Sheila. She's nineteen, I think. She also goes university

Taseen Khan

- 13 -

and, if that weren't enough, she also has a job! Two things to do in one day! She's awesome but crazy as well.

Anyhow, since I have told you about one family member let me tell you about the rest.

My mum is a full-time housewife, who looks after us all day.

My dad is a cab driver during the night so he sleeps through the day. Can you see the difference between him and my mum?

Next on the list is my brother Imran; he's fifteen and acts like a gangster. I find it completely irrelevant. He has his GCSEs coming up as well but he says he doesn't care. Also no one takes the time to care for him and his education because everyone pretty much has their own things to do.

Now let's talk about Tamriq. At the age of thirteen all he does is play on the computer non-stop all day. (The geek has nothing else to do all day).

Taseen Khan

Let's talk about my little baby sister Leila who is six and is very cute. But don't be baffled by her face – what's inside is a heart of evil doing naughtiness. But hell she's cute.

Now, it's time to talk about me. My name is Tanveer Ahmed Khan. I am eleven years old and am awesome. I don't mean to brag but I'm probably the cutest, smartest and most charming of us all. I mean, who gets chosen for a 'Gifted & Talented course' nowadays, eh? I got chosen because I was the cleverest in my whole school, and again I don't mean to brag.

It is Monday morning, meaning time for school. I wake up at seven forty-five, but I was so tired, that's when I made my cereal. Instead of sugar I put salt. I didn't realise it at first but when I put it in my mouth, that's when the bitter taste started to kick in. Erghhh.

After that, my mum was shrieking her head off that we were going to be late for school if we didn't hurry up. By the way my mum can't actually speak English. However, as she is from Bangladesh she can speak Bengali. But my dad

Taseen Khan

can speak English, a little bit. It's pretty difficult like this as whenever anyone says anything, my mum wouldn't really understand.

As soon as we left home, my mum bumped into one of her Bengali friends. We all walked to school together, until they had this conversation in Bengali about what secondary school I was going. But I'll translate it for you.

"So, what school are you sending your child to?" asked my mum's friend.

"I'll be sending my child Tanveer to Earnshaw secondary school, the school I send all my children to. Anyway, why'd you ask?" said my mum.

"Well Tanveer is one of the brightest kids in the school, and I'm sending my daughter to a private school for a scholarship. But she has to take some tests first to get in." she said.

"First of all, my Tanveer is the brightest in the school, not 'one of the brightest', all right? And

Taseen Khan

so, so what about private schools, what do you want me to do?" said my mum.

"Well get your son into a private school!"

My mum looked at me, and then I looked at her. I knew I had a choice to make.

After school, I came home with my mum. She was looking at me like she was expecting something. I didn't know what. When we arrived home my dad came straight up to me and stared at me looking for an answer. (By the way this was the first time he was awake during the day.) After a few seconds it shot to my head like a bullet: the choice. I hadn't thought about it but I knew I had to give him an answer.

"I don't know, dad. I haven't decided yet." I answered nervously.

"Okay son, I'll tell your mum that you are going to try." He said.

"Yeah okay dad, you go ahead … Wait, what, no – I said I don't know, oh daaad," I screamed.

Taseen Khan

I was baffled because I hadn't made a choice, but, my dad said I did. Well that's my dad for you.

After that the whole family rushed to the kitchen with a plate. It was lunch time. I was second in queue and the smell of the food was blowing me away. After we all had got our food of soft, tender basmati rice and juicy, chewy lamb, we all rushed around the house to different places to eat. Some in the kitchen, some in bedrooms and I was in the sitting room.

The sitting room was the best place to eat. Nice relaxing sofas, an eighteen-inch television and a beautiful Sky HD box. It was awesome.

Straight after dinner I heard some talking. It was my older sister Sheila on the phone. I heard a few things like, 'When are you going to tell her?' or 'Do you have the money.' I knew she was up to something.

When my sister came out of the room I asked her what was she up to.

Taseen Khan

"None of your business, nerd!" she replied thunderously.

She then kicked the heater and had a conversation with my mum in Bengali but, again, here's the translation:
"Mum … I … uh …wanna get married. To a man called Syeed," said my sister.

"Wow. Yes, yes. First, though, what country is he from huh? Is he smart, handsome? Come on then answer." My mum said whilst in the process of making tea.

"Kind … very kind, did I mention he was kind? Wait, wait brave, brave, brave, brave and Pakistan and uh, brave," said my sister Sheila.

"NO! NO! He has to be Bengali! And that's final, now go to your room!" my mum screamed.

"But muuuuum! I'm a grown-up now **I CAN MAKE MY OWN DECISIONS!**" she bellowed.

Taseen Khan

"No. It's up to me, your mother. I shall decide who you marry." Said mum.

By the way, my mum said heaps and heaps of stuff about what kind of man my sister will be marrying. But just for you, I'm not going to say what she said. (If you really want to know, I guess I'm sorry).

After the conversation my mum was angry. I could tell she was angry because she dropped a teacup. That's when I decided to stay out of her way for the whole day.

After a while, I heard noises coming from the room so I went to check it out. Then, there standing in front of me was a hacked-off sister, who was packing her bags and taking mum and dads secret stash of money.

"What are you doing?! That's mum and dad's money. Where are you going? What's happening?" I said.

"First of all, SHUT UP! Second of all, don't tell anyone," she said.

Taseen Khan

"Don't tell anyone what?" I said.

"That I'm running away. I'm going to go to live with Syeed. I'll phone home, Tanveer, as soon as I can. But don't worry about me, I'll be safe," she said softly.

Her voice seemed to calm me down. She gave one final kiss then said goodbye. I hugged her and I just couldn't let go. I let go when she really had to leave.

She exited through the balcony.

When she left, the room went dark and cold. I was frightened.

I ran to the bed and started crying, swearing and punching everything soft. Then, out of nowhere standing in front of me was Imran; he also was packing his bags.

"Are you running away?", I asked.

Taseen Khan

"He, what's it got to do wiv you blud? And anyways FAM, why da hell would I do a runner?" he replied.

I was getting a bit suspicious, but I didn't want to poke my nose in his business or he would've probably beaten the hell out of me.

Then I noticed my mum was crying and I also heard my sister Sheila's voice. She must've rung home already.

A few seconds later, I heard a big bang. My mum broke a plate.

Two minutes later, exactly two minutes later, my dad entered. (For the first time he worked during the day … unbelievable!) He asked me what all the fuss was about and when I told him everything, he went straight to my mum. The fight began.

Arguing, plate crashing, violence and  Swearing in Bengali.

Taseen Khan

I started crying so badly that my tears would've probably been enough to clean Buckingham Palace's floors.

Also, my dad started blaming everything on my mum, like if she wasn't alive, none of this would've happened. It's not only my mum's fault, though. I mean, if my dad 'the bat' spent more time with us then at work maybe none of this would've happened. He then started talking about this so called "society" and he started asking what they would think. Who on earth is this so called society person? I mean, who cares about what other people think! After a heated argument, he left the house.

My mum was in tears and the whole house was in darkness. There was no light, no happiness and no hope left.

Knock, knock. My mum answered it and there standing in front of us was a police officer with Imran.

"Madam, your little mischievous boy has been caught drug-dealing on the streets of Layman

Taseen Khan

Way. Therefore, he shall be going to community service or, if he's unlucky, he'll get locked up," said the officer fiercely.

I had to explain to my mum, and as soon as I did she fainted.

"Uhhhh, get off me. I swear down blud. Huh feds! Ten years later bruv we are gonna be the police. My generation. So you man better watch what you do FAM," Imran cried.

He was frustrated and he was trying to escape but he had no chance.

I then called the ambulance. Before the ambulance got here, my mum got up and said she'd take the matter to court.

As soon as the ambulance arrived, they said everything was fine. They then started saying is everything okay in my mum's life and stuff like that. My mum didn't understand but the ambulance said they were going to get counselling help. But I know we don't need them.

Taseen Khan

After a few minutes my mum called me, Leila and Tamriq to the sitting room. In Bengali she said that we children cannot tell anyone in the community about what happened today or else.

We all replied, saying 'yes'. But I knew someone would eventually tell someone.

I was right. The next day at school my little stupid sister told all the teachers. Ayayayaayayayyayyayay! We are all going to get in trouble for this.

I was right again! My mum said we should've taken more responsibility. However, what could I have done? I mean, did she expect me to stay under Leila's tail all day!?

After that she said what about the "Society" and what they would say. Who is this so called "Society" … Who?

On Saturday morning, the counselling arrived. They were talking to my mum and dad for two hours, and were still going. I couldn't hear what they were saying because the door was locked.

Taseen Khan

For a moment, it seemed like all the bad luck in the world had chosen to stay at our house. After a while my mum opened the door and I saw my dad signing documents. He then told the lady how pleased he was with her service. The good news, or should I say the excellent news, is that according to the law my brother isn't going jail; he's just going to be kept under observation for a short while at the detention centre. This means both of my parents will have to go court, plus they have been given a warning (whatever that is).

Usually after something like this my dad would run riot. But today he seems all calm. It seems to me that something is changing his behaviour.

It was now eight am and my mum was cooking breakfast as usual.

I went up to my mum and asked her in Bengali: "You know the private school that I'm going to, mum? Have you sent the application forms?"

"No, not yet. But hopefully I will do tomorrow," she replied.

Taseen Khan

As we were going to school Tamriq, "the nerdy one", asked my mum for thirty pounds for books. I mean, who nowadays spends thirty pounds on book. I knew it was for that new Call of Duty game. But I don't grass up on people. So basically I'm letting him off. I usually wouldn't but Imran taught me a really intense, hard lesson on grassing. You know what I mean.

When I came home I could smell the deep-fried vegetable samosa flying with the atmosphere around the house. Suddenly all my senses (even my sixth) stopped dead in their tracks; the phone was ringing. I knew it was my sister, it must be my sister.

I was wrong. It was my aunty Rowza from Cardiff. She asked me if everyone was all right. But I told her everyone is stressed because my sister ran away and because Imran was in trouble with the police. She then told me to give the phone to my mum.

Five minutes later, tears of anger and no hope were falling from my mum's eyes.

Taseen Khan

I went to watch television because I knew the conversation was going to be looooong.

As I entered the room, guess who was there? My dad! He said the counsellors told him to stay more at home then at work. So we've decided to play cricket in our living room whilst Leila was asleep, Tamriq was playing on his PS3. We were enjoying it a lot until my dad said:

"Did you print out the application forms for your entry exams?"

"No, dad. But since you are at home, let's do it together. I've applied for Earnshaw, the normal one, Ashley Hill Boys' and Einstein Liver School." I answered.

I don't really see differences between standard and so called "private" schools. To me, they're all the same, just plain old schools.

You know, it was actually fun with my dad. This vibe made me feel ecstatic. I mean he understood way more than my mum. I want to spend time with him more often.

Taseen Khan

After we completed the forms, my dad wrote a cheque for the two private schools. Can you believe that it cost like three hundred pounds including the books I needed to study. Because of this I must pass the exams.

After a week I received a letter from the schools both of them, saying practically the same thing: when the exam will be held and that I'll be taking verbal reasoning, non-verbal reasoning, and maths and English tests.

I mean, what is this reasoning stuff? I was never taught it at primary. What is it?? I can officially say I was shocked and gutted.

I had to do something; I mean, the books weren't helping me get smarter at all.

I didn't know what to do. But then I got it. I went to my house phone and searched up my sister Sheila's number.

She must, must, know a thing or two about the tests. I mean she has been learning for like all her life. She's the one who knows the answers.

Taseen Khan

When I talked to her it turned out she knew nothing about verbal and non-verbal reasoning! But she suggested I hire tutors. Then she said to print out past papers.

The papers seemed hard but I knew I couldn't tell my dad or I would get a BBS: Bengali back slap. And let's just say that I really hate those …

I decided to ring my sister again in the morning to see if she was all right. Halfway through the conversation my dad entered. I quickly hung up.

"Who you talking to?", he said

I did not know what to say. But I said something. Me and my mouth, urghhhh.

"My best friend Taseen," I replied

"Son, if I was you I wouldn't talk to him, he's a bad influence. Talk to Takbeer, he is a better boy," he said

"Yeah okay," I said

Taseen Khan

I was still in stress. I had no option to tell my dad I need a tutor.

As I approached my dad, I was sweating more than five bottles of water. But I had to do it.

I told him the books he provided me were no good. Then I told him we weren't taught about this stuff at school and I found it very difficult.

I mean, I knew he wouldn't be able to afford it because, at the end of the day, we are in poverty. We live in social housing, we practically live off benefits, and my dad gets minimum wage.

After a week my dad said he met someone whilst working. Apparently that person is a tutor and he offered to teach me for fifteen pounds an hour.

Sometimes I hated it. I wished we had enough money so that I could buy a bike, get a new pair of trainers, and get a wide-screen television. I mean I don't even have P.E. clothes. But I really want some designer gear. But we can't afford it. Silly me for dreaming.

Taseen Khan

I know that both of my parents are very emotional and upset after what my sister and brother did. They are ashamed to show their face in the local community now. I mean almost everyone gossips about my family. But I told my parents not to worry about it. Why? Because I believe we should forget about recent events and move forward in our lives.

I feel confident now because I had those extra classes.

Every single student applying was in the hall. And boy was the hall big. It's like the size of my primary.

I was getting a bit embarrassed because everyone was wearing suits with expensive shoes. But I was wearing a jumper and baggy pair of trousers. My dad was wearing a random of top and pair of trousers. Tamriq and Leila were at the next-door neighbour's house. Oh yeah, I almost forgot, and I really hope I do. My mum was wearing a sari. I felt embarrassed, really embarrassed.

Taseen Khan

After a few minutes some English women tried to get a conversation with my mum. But I had to interrupt and say my mum couldn't speak English. This meant she started a BORING, conversation with me. I mean I'm not even going to tell you about it. I mean all this happened whilst my dad was sleeping. Yeah, awkward.

It was around two pm now and the headmaster entered. He went on and started saying things like 'Don't be worried' and 'It's an easy paper'. All I wanted to do was hit him. He then told our parents to go home and come back at four pm. My mum and dad came to me and wished me good luck. They know I hate their kisses so they didn't dare to kiss me. Bleurghhh. Even thinking about it makes me sick

As I entered the room there was this tense feeling.

"To pass the exam if you are applying for a scholarship you need ninety percent. And if you are going to pay fees you need seventy per cent. You may start the exam," said the teacher.

Taseen Khan

That's when I heard one hundred pages flick.

Two weeks later …

It was Saturday now and I was feeling anxious. The results from all the schools were going to come through the post today.

As soon as I got the letters I opened them all at the same time and I was… not in. I failed. Only joking! Obviously I'd get in, yipeeeee!

This was a happy moment in our family. I couldn't believe what I saw. I got into every single private school.

My dad said I made his dreams come true. Then he said he knew it would never be too late to achieve your educational dreams.

Now it was time to think what school to go to. I really didn't know, private school or Earnshaw? The only thing that came to my mind was: can my family adjust to the posh people and their society? I don't know. Then I had my choice. I

Taseen Khan

mean, I don't want my family to feel isolated in the 'rich world'.

So, Earnshaw, here I come …

Lovely to read Taseen's book. He is a very talented boy. I wish him all the success in the future.

*Barbara Hughes MBE*
*Ex councillor and Ex Mayor of London Borough of Camden*

Taseen Khan

## Cllr Sarah Hayward, Leader of Camden Council

"I feel immensely privileged to have been asked to endorse Taseen's book. What a talented young man he is.

"The stories he has written are wise and perceptive way beyond his young age. They are funny, bittersweet and offer a touching and humorous insight into modern life.

"I thoroughly recommend this collection of short stories and hope Taseen keeps writing. Even when he's playing football (or cricket) for England ."

Taseen Khan

# The second story
## My life in London

Please look at Glossary, certain words Taseen used to make this story funny.


Olymfics- Olympics
Underfants- Underpants
Airfort- Airport
Flane-Plan
Farents- Parents
Ve-We
Vent-Went
Vhich-Which
Vukinkam falice – Buckingham Palace
Towler Brich-Tower Bridge
Fig fen- Big Ben
Englesh-English


Taseen Khan

Hi! My name is Chatpul Patel. I am I think nine years old. I and my family are coming from India to Londen for the Olymfics. I can't really speak Englesh properly and so cant my family.

We live in India in a house. It's not ours. It is actually my dad's boss's house. He loves us and my family. He was very to offer us to go to Londen to see the Olymfics as a treat. How awesome ….

It took me half an hour to pack my suitcase. It consisted of fourteen plain white t-shirts, fourteen tracksuit bottoms, ten vests, and ten pairs of socks, ten underpants and this locket of a baby inside. I found the locket about a week ago and nobody can tell me what it is. By the way I got fourteen pairs of every-ting and ten pairs of underfants and that for the two weeks of the Olymfics. Clever, eh?

At the New Delhi Airfort it vas scary. I had never been on a flane before. As ve vent in the Airfort our boss waved us goodbye. My farents then went to the British Airways check thing and gave our passports. It was funny seeing my picture on something. Hehe.

As ve vere entering the flane I kissed the locket vhich I now called my good luck charm. We then entered the flane. We then vent through this tunnel. It vas veird. In the plane ve sat at the economy seats or something. The British Airways people then put our luggage on somewhere at the top.

As ve vere lifting of, my tummy had this funny feeling. But I actually liked it.

The flane also had a radio I think, a desk and a pocket. I was listening to Hindi FM. They were 'busting out' a tune called 'Om Shanti Om', my favourite tune. And I also learnt that I should pronounce w with a w not a v. Hehe embarrassing.

When lunch came they gave us rice and a meat. Apparently my parents asked for it. Well, my mum did. I and my dad were then complaining for chapatti. However, the people did not give us what we wanted. Thanks a lot, British Airways.

Taseen Khan

The flight was apparently another ten hours longer. Damn. We also stopped at Dubai. Almost everyone on the flane went out and came back with McDonalds or toys. But we really couldn't afford it.

I mean, when we arrived at London we are going to stay in our cousins' house. We got tickets to every single event. Well, the first round of every event except the finals of the football. I can't wait.

When were about an hour from Heathrow Airport, I was getting nervous. I mean my first time in London – what would happen?

At the airport my cousins rang us to say they were here to pick us up. They live in Right Ruislip. It's only a ten minute drive from the airport apparently.

When we got off the flane we couldn't find our luggages. We searched and searched for them until we found only three out of four. We couldn't find our luggage full of food. But they said that they'd deliver it to us tomorrow.

Taseen Khan

As we got out of the airport we all went on my uncle's Mercedes-Benz. It was cool. I mean, I never see those types of car in India.

I also couldn't wait to kick-start my journey as a London boy.

When we got in the house it was big. I mean it had stairs and a something like a sixty inch TV. In India ours was eighteen inch. And our boss is one of the richest in the whole of India.

My parents were going to stay in bedroom two and me in bedroom three with my cousin. He is cool. He has a forty eight inch TV in his own room. He also has a PS3 I think, the whole collection of Call of Duty (I think that's how you pronounce it) and a TV Sky box or something. It was like heaven.

It was my first night in Londen and I couldn't sleep. I don't know why? My cousin was just playing on his PS3 and he said that it's the time difference.

Taseen Khan

It turns out he was right. I fell asleep at ten pm. The time everyone woke up. This also meant that I woke up at seven pm. I eat something called cereals pops. It was nice, that's all I could say.

In the second night of Londen I thought I needed to dream then I'd be able to sleep. I started dreaming about the locket for some reason.

It took me to some sort of flashback. Like when I was around two. My mum had a big belly and she went into room sixteen. I was with my dad. After about two minutes my mum walked out and she was crying and her belly looked like it had been popped. I didn't know or understand anything.

Then I heard an explosion and I woke up. It was ten pm. But I swear I was dreaming for two minutes. Wow, this is crazy. And when I looked to my right my cousin was playing that Call of Duty game, hence the explosion.

During breakfast I couldn't stop thinking about the locket. So I and my cousin went to the sitting room. I told him all about my dream. He said just

Taseen Khan

to try and forget about it and play some Call of Duty.

It worked. He was awesome at it. He killed me like eighty times. Then we played football. I beat him something like six nil. I'm really rubbish at football games. I should've got at least fifteen goals. I mean I was even the three stars, West Ham team and he was Spain. He told me that Spain is two stars. I can't believe it.

After playing for about two hours, it was time for me and my family to go out. We went to have a tour around Londen. Then we would come back home and watch the Olymfics opening ceremony.

Londen is officially amazing. We saw: the Queen's house vukinkam falice (I think), towler brich, fig fen, a lion and Westfield. Westfield has got to be the best place there. There's: shops, cinemas and yam yam.....fast foods....I' m loving it.

When we arrived back at Right Ruislip, my parents and I were telling everyone about our day. For about two minutes. And I don't

Taseen Khan

get that because we were out for seven hours!

It was ceremony time. It was, I think, nine pm. We all got some snacks, sat on the sofa then started to watch.

Half an hour later … I and my cousin were playing on the PS3 and everyone downstairs was watching a Bollywood movie.

I mean, no offence, but it was boring. All I saw was basically a big Voldemort and that's it. Oh yeah and err the cricket of Englishmen. It was what my cousin would call it "dead".

It was the third night of Londen. Instead of sleeping I decided to play Call of Duty all night until like four am. It was good. The bombs and bullets kept me alive.

When it was finally time to sleep I was just thinking about my dream. Next thing you know, it's the morning and I'm eating cereal pops.

Taseen Khan

How does this happen so fast? Someone please, please tell me.

We were beginning our fourth day in Londen. Another thirteen and something like that days left till we go back to India.

Today we were going to see diving. You know what? To save time I'll tell you all the events I'm going to every day: so, first is diving, second day basketball, third day hammer throw, fourth day javelin, fifth day tennis, sixth day shooting to watch our gold boy Abhinav Bindra, seventh day wrestling to see another homeboy Sushil Kumar try and reclaim us bronze again, eighth day badminton to watch home girl Saina Newhal, ninth day to watch another home girl Mary Kom beat other women in boxing, tenth day Judo, eleventh day rowing, twelfth day table tennis, thirteenth day one hundred metre sprint and on the fourteenth day the football finals. Then we'd watch the closing ceremony and after that we'd be back in India.

Taseen Khan

Day one of Olympics …

Today we were going to see diving; I didn't
 really like that sport much. But it's an
 Olympic event! We decided to take my
 cousin along to all of our Olympic events
 because they were short of attendance or
 something. (Staying in Londen has already
 improved all my Englesh! I mean I don't
 even say Olymfics any more. Haha!) We
 were seeing some British guy who almost
 everyone expected to win gold called Tom
 Daley, diving. He was pretty good. I think
 he did like a twist and a flip or something
 like that in midair. After a while I started
 looking around the stadium. When I saw
 two Islamic people that had full beards and
 that were digging in their bags I got scared.
 People have been telling me there could be
 bombings and that. I was getting the creeps.
 But I knew they weren't going to do
 anything. I respect all religions and that.
 But it's just these fake YouTube videos that
 probably give me the creeps or something. I
 mean, I don't know. I couldn't believe it as

Taseen Khan

well; all they got out was sandwich. It made me feel peckish.

I told my mum and she passed the Indian popcorn around, or should I say "samosas".

It was stuffed with lamb bits and sweet corn. I loved it!

The diving was pretty boring. It also lasted like three hours or something. I just started to play with my cousins IiPod. It's touch screen or something. I played a game called Angry Birds and I couldn't stop.

At the end of the diving I don't know who won because I was playing Angry Birds through out. But I do know Tom Daley qualified to the finals or something.

So far I have not been impressed with the Olympics. It's all been too boring. But tomorrow we were going to see basketball. And guess who we were going to watch play? The American dream's team are in their first game against France. I knew it

Taseen Khan

would be entertaining but all that's happening tomorrow.

It is my fourth night in Londen. This time I decided to think about me being a WWE superstar. It actually helped and I managed to get good sleep. However, I still needed to pluck up the courage and ask my parents about the locket. (By the way, I just realised that Londen isn't Right Ruislip, it's Middlesex? I'm getting real confused).

Anyways, today we were going to see the basketball match. I knew America was going to win, and guess what? I was wrong. I'm joking, I was right! America won ninety-eight to seventy-one! It was full of goals galore. I mean, only if football was like that.

When we got back home my cousin said let's watch Eastenders. It was a British everyday life drama, and boy it was addictive. I started watching every other episode over the past seven days on BBC iPplayer. It's a pretty cool site. I watched so many things.

Taseen Khan

My fifth night in Londen, Wait Ruislip, Wait
Right Ruislip was coming up.

Tonight, I was going to think about being an
actor. It worked. For a few minutes,
then I decided to be a basketball
player. Well, I think I was and boy
was I good!

This meant the next day I started trying all the
skills and shots I scored in my dream
in the garden. I failed. Yeah. Turns
out, it was just a dream.

So now it was time to go and see the hammer
throw. I think my WWE dream was a
sign. I mean, I don't know what I'm
going to see until the morning when
my mum finally tells me. Look, WWE
have strong, bulky men fighting and
tossing each other around and the
hammer throw has strong, bulky men
throwing things around. What's the
difference?

Taseen Khan

Yeah, turns out we were watching the women's
hammer throw. I mean, don't get me
wrong. It was entertaining and the
noise that the women made when
throwing the hammer throw kept me
from sleeping.

I don't know what happened, mainly because I
couldn't read the writing on the board.
The other days my cousin tagged
along so I knew what the scores were.
However, my cousin didn't come
today because he had a really bad
stomach ache. I think it was the hot
chilly he had yesterday that caused
this. But hey, that's just my thoughts.

I definitely knew that Russian women with abs
and huge biceps went through to the
next round, though. Her name was …
You know what? I don't even know
how to pronounce it so I'm not going
to bother. But boy was she good at
throwing a hammer, wait no it's a ball
right? That's why I don't get the
Olympics. It's a ball that they're

Taseen Khan

throwing, but they call it the 'hammer throw'. Awkward.

As soon as I got home I felt bored and decided to prank my cousin. I threw a Olympic mascot at him whilst hiding in his cupboard. It was so funny until I heard him cry.

My parents and his parents told us to take more care and that. I really didn't care though. I mean, that's the way of teenage- hood, right?

A few days had passed. I watched my fellow Indians compete in the Olympics and they did all right.

It was finally the time, though, to watch the football finals. However, I couldn't go. I had this really bad cold and it would only get worse if I went.

So, my family decided to go without me. That's strange, right? That meant I had the pleasure of watching it at home with

Taseen Khan

my uncle and aunt. Oh yeah, my
cousin was there too. It got boring at
the end because you don't feel that
vibe you get when you are at the
stadium.

I took a deep sigh and plucked up the courage to
ask my parents about the locket when
they come back.

I was feeling nervous but I wanted to know all
about the locket. It was like a
temptation, an unanswered guilt.

When they came home I went straight in. In front
of everyone, I asked them so that they'd
give me an answer and not just forget what
I said.

They looked at me like I had just killed someone.

Then they left me there thinking. What was going
on?

You know, staying in London has made me learn
a lot of things and has made me realise

Taseen Khan

about life on a whole new level. It has educated me, it has made me feel like I'm part of this country and I just don't want to leave.

It was my last night in London before I left for India at six thirty pm.

We had lots of food, like loads, a big hugging ceremony and prize giving to me.

My cousin gave me an iPod and I loved him for that.

When we got to the airport everything was intense but when we got on the plane I wanted to just run back home to Right Ruislip.

But it was too late now, the plane had lifted off.

It was around ten pm now and almost everyone was asleep except for me and my mum. That's when she said to me in Hindu (I'm translating it for you in English):"Listen Chatpul, that locket is the picture of your baby brother. He's dead. As soon as he came out, we took pictures and had a

Taseen Khan

laugh, one hour later, he's breathing just stopped during the night. Never lose that locket Chatpul, never."

Tears were running down my eyes like it was a waterfall. I couldn't sleep. I just wish that my baby brother was alive now and you know what, I'd give my life for him to have a second chance in life. You know if it ever comes to that, I'll never back down. I love baby brother no matter if you're dead, or not.

Taseen's book is a delight. Witty and wise, it's hard to believe he's just 12. I very much look forward to hearing more from Taseen in the future.

Very best wishes,

*Katie Matthews*
*Community Engagement Manager*
*The Francis Crick Institute*

Taseen Khan

# Play 1

## THE ITCHY
## BLOOD CURE
By Taseen Khan, aged 10

CHARACTERS:
Adidas – A Vampire Clown
Bary Am – An Elephant with an itchy bum,
looking for a cure


Dramaturged by Ross Mullan
20/06/2010
© 2010 Scene & Heard

Taseen Khan- a writer extraordinary……..
I read this book and I find Taseen's writings so full of creativity, great adult humour for someone of 12 years; insight into human failings and gentle humour about those around him in this world he sees so clearly. The stories and plays encompassed in this book were so very funny, descriptive and with an obvious in-depth understanding of society and the community around him. I enjoyed reading his book and look forward to many more years of creativity and brilliant works from this young man with a great future in the world of literature. I am proud he is a local resident and active in Scene and Heard working with other children to create original theatre.

*Councillor Roger Robinson, OBE*
*Ward councillor- St Pancras and Somers*
*Town Ward, Camden Council.*

Taseen Khan

# SCENE ONE

## TIME
In the future, the year 203
2.31pm

## PLACE
Madam Tussaud's (sign please)

## AT RISE
Adidas is doing James Bond
impersonations/poses. In a James Bond outfit.
Barry Am enters from the toilet.

## BARRY AM
*(Scratching her bum)*
Rubbish! James Bond is just a fake character. I'm
not a fan because Jackie Chan is way better.

## ADIDAS
Do you wanna get shot? And anyway, why would
you be a Jackie Chan fan, you're too fat.

Taseen Khan

## BARRY AM
Oh I thought you were just a Madame Tussaud wax figure and anyway you don't have the right to look at my belly because this is my body and no one looks at it but me.
*(Scratches her bum)*

## ADIDAS
Whoa! Don't touch me! What did you scratch your bum for?

## BARRY AM
*(Turn to the audience & says)*
I had some chilli and now I'm not allowed to have it 'cause the doctor said "Chilli will make my bum even itchier and the only cure is clown blood".
*(She has a little laugh and scratches her bum)*

## ADIDAS
What are you saying? 'Cause if you're talking about me I'll show you some karate. Do you have a disease or something cause I do too? My name is Adidas *(puts his hand out to shake)* and I'm a James Bond Impersonator slash half vampire half clown.

Taseen Khan

## BARRY AM

My name is Barry Am and I am a kungephant,
which is a kung fu elephant.

*(She puts her hand out to shake, then pulls it*
*away and says:)*
No hand contact.

*(She pulls out a syringe and says:)*
Gimme some clown blood. I need it for my cure
for the itchy bum.

*(Scratches her bum)*
Ooh! Oh! Ooh!

## ADIDAS

Whoa! Whoa! Whoa! Put that back! Or I will tell
this to the police and you'll be sent to American
prison by plane.

## BARRY AM

You can't do that – I am scared of planes.

*(Scratches her bum)*
Ooh, oh, ooh.

Taseen Khan

## ADIDAS
Well, I'm scared of injections.

## BARRY AM
Well maybe we can sort this out, what do you want? And whatever it is I will help you with it. As long as you help me with my want, which is to let me inject you and let me have your <u>clown</u> blood.

*(Scratches her bum)*
Ooh why does my bum always itch?

## ADIDAS
I will help you with your want but I need a few days to prepare. But first things first, help me with my thing; you see my thing is to just be a single person and not a half Clown half vampire. My father is a "keep out" sign called Simon Cowell and he is very strict and he lives in Saudi Arabia. I don't want to be like my dad, I want to be a gentle "come in" sign.

## BARRY AM
Where is Saudi Arabia? Is Simon Cowell from X-Factor your real dad?

Taseen Khan

## ADIDAS

No, no, no, it's just a name his mum gave him 'cause he is so strict. I don't know where Saudi Arabia is but I think it's in North America.

## BARRY AM

Well, I have a mother who is quicksand and always trying to lose weight and a brother who is a banana phone who always makes prank calls. Silly family right? But unfortunately they are all in Canada but I do have a pet banana called Manana. And I always confuse him with my brother.

## ADIDAS

I have a pet called Cocoa who is a half-eaten chocolate bar and I accidently ate the other half. I do feel sorry for him but who cares?
Okay, let's go back to the real talk. Now you know my wants. How are you going to help me?

## BARRY AM

What's the cure for yours?

Taseen Khan

# BARRY AM & ADIDAS
Thinking time!

*(Pacing back and forth)*

## BARRY AM
*(Stops pacing and does a Kung Fu pose)*
Do you know the ancient art of kung fu? 'Cause maybe I can punch one of your heads so you only have one head.

## ADIDAS
Okay I admit it! I'm afraid of kung fu!

## BARRY AM
*(Bursts out in a really crazy laugh – high, low, evil, and weird)*
Sorry, that was just a little moment, let me catch my breath. So are you sticking with the kung fu idea or not?

## ADIDAS
You see, that's what I will have to think about because I might end up in hospital and anyway, can't I just have plastic surgery?

Taseen Khan

## BARRY AM
But with plastic surgery you could be hated
'cause that's what happened to Michael Jackson.
Look there he is ...

*(She points to the wax figure of M.J.)*

Look at the golden words of the statue. It says
M.J. has done plastic surgery and turned white!

## ADIDAS
I don't want to be hated and so I will just stick
with your idea but I need a few days to prepare
for the injection so let me exercise for a few days
and then you'll see me with guns.

*(He kisses his muscles, lifts his claws and it goes
to dark)*

Taseen Khan

'Taseen Khan is an amazing writer. The stories were full of variety and had has laughing, crying, in tears and full of varying emotions. My 9 year old son and I were thoroughly amused by them.

Taseen's writing skills can entertain people of all ages and leave you wanting more. I would highly recommend this book to everyone'

*Councillor Nasim Ali OBE*
*Cabinet Member for Young People*
*London Borough of Camden*

I'm very happy to endorse Taseen's book. Reading the book took me back to a place I'd forgotten - my childhood fantasies where amazing things can happen and be described. I particularly liked the visit to No 10 Frowning Street - perhaps we can get it renamed! Best of luck to Taseen and I'm looking forward to see him on "Meet the Author".
*Paul Tomlinson*
*Local resident*

Taseen Khan

# SCENE TWO

## TIME
Two days after normal time

## PLACE
Adidas' home

## AT RISE
He is showing his house to Barry Am.


## ADIDAS
Welcome to my home. Here's my hexagon-shaped football mansion, the size of a stadium. Here's my coffin made out of balloons and covered in red noses. And Cocoa sleeps in that fan there in case he melts.

## BARRY AM
Whoa! My home is way bigger! I live in a diamond ring, and I sleep in a bath with seven pillows. And Manana sleeps in the sink. Okay, time to get on with the cures.

## ADIDAS

Taseen Khan

Wait a minute. For your cure you're going to inject me and for my cure you're going to knock my head off so end of the day I'm the one who is going to get beaten up.

## BARRY AM
But who cares?

## ADIDAS
But I think I have a cure for mine. You can inject me but you can't knock my head off so instead you can paint me into a "come in" sign. But I have four words for you first: "It better be good".

## BARRY AM
Okay, let's start the painting. Okay, now rest your head and take a few deep breaths. Okay, close your eyes as you take this deep breath.

## ADIDAS
*(Closes his eyes & starts snoring)*
*(She takes out the syringe and injects him. Adidas screams!)*

Ahhhhh!

Taseen Khan

## BARRY AM
Ha, got you! Now time for me to drink it.

## ADIDAS
Wow I've got claws everywhere. I'm becoming a vampire. I am a single person finally.

## BARRY AM
*(Has turned into a clown)*
And I am a clown elephant with no itchy bum. Thank you for this. I owe you my friend.

## ADIDAS
You know that "come in" sign that you were about to paint. I've decided that I would rather be just a vampire.

## BARRY AM
Well done you have finally become a single person. It's okay that you're a vampire as long as you don't bite anyone, and if you do I'm still a kung fu master you know.

Taseen Khan

## ADIDAS

Okay, now you can handshake me cause you don't scratch your bum anymore.

*(They shake hands)*

I know well Taseen's Primary School, Edith Neville, and the Somers Town theatrical mentoring project Scene & Heard, and these stories show how a bright young person can value and use such marvellous resources and begin to focus his clearly exceptional talents!

*Esther Caplin, Chair of Governors, Edith Neville Primary School .*

Taseen Khan

# Play 2

# HIGHWAY SPLIT
By Taseen Khan, aged 10

## CHARACTERS:
Wackstar – A cockroach highwaywoman
Shut – A banana skin
A cockroach prime minister


Dramaturged by David Cottis
12th & 13th March

© 2011 Scene & Heard

I have worked with Taseen over the past few years at Scene & Heard and it has been a pleasure to observe the development and growing sophistication of his playwriting. What an absolute delight it is now to read Taseen's book - the voice of a young man living in London . His personality shines through his words. His writing is rich with creativity and he displays an openness and honesty that is both disarming and charming. I look forward to seeing what he will do next with his imagination, his enthusiasm and his charm.

*Rosalind Paul*
*Artistic Director*
*Scene & Heard*

Taseen Khan

# SCENE ONE

## TIME
4.30pm

## PLACE
Inside SHUT'S bin

## AT RISE
SHUT is there, doing a funny dance and singing a funny song.

## SHUT
*(sings)*
Yo, yo, yo. My name is Shut. My dad's called U.G. and he looks like a butt.

So, how do you make a witch itch? Take the W away. (*Drum roll*)
And because I think you're kind people, I'll tell you another joke. How do you wake up Lady Gaga? Poke her in the face (*Drum roll*)

Taseen Khan

(Enter Wackstar. She bursts through the doors
and interrupts him)

**WACKSTAR**
And now, who dares to stand against me?

**SHUT**
Ah, it's a highwayman!
(*SHUT runs away and hides in a corner.*
*WACKSTAR walks slowly to the corner he's in*)

**WACKSTAR**
Come on, then, pick your sword up and fight!

**SHUT**
I don't have a sword, and how did you get into
my bin house, highwayman?

**WACKSTAR**
I'm a woman, actually, and I think you're going
to need to repair your window.

**SHUT**
Anyway, how dare you interrupt my practice
time? I'm on a strict schedule. I'm on the road to

Taseen Khan

becoming a comedian. Why did you become a highwayman?

**WACKSTAR**
First of all, I'm a woman, and second of all, as a cockroach, I believe tiny people can do big things. So all you people who didn't believe a cockroach could become a highwayman, be careful.

**SHUT**
I thought you were a woman?

**WACKSTAR**
Look what you've done, you banana peel, you confused me. Now I don't know the difference between what I am. Anyways, why were you scared of me?

**SHUT**
Because once a highwayman threatened me, and told me to answer all the questions he asked.

**WACKSTAR**
Didn't he try to rob you?

Taseen Khan

**SHUT**
No it was a 'pressurising' highwayman, and believe me, some of those questions were really weird

**WACKSTAR**
So you're trying to become a comedian?

**SHUT**
Yeah, I wanna perform in the Apollo show alongside Michael McIntyre, and I'm just gonna scream 'cause I've got a long way to go. So cover your ears.

**WACKSTAR**
Don't worry, I've heard a lot of screaming in my life.

**SHUT**
How?

**WACKSTAR**
Because I've killed 1,567people *(waves her sword)* so you better be careful, because I'm one of the best highwaymen this cruel world has ever seen.

Taseen Khan

**SHUT**

I know, because of the leader's wrong decision, it's become a cruel world.

**WACKSTAR**

How dare you say that about my man!

**SHUT**

Who's your man?

**WACKSTAR**

The prime minister of the cockroach world

**SHUT**

Isn't he married?

**WACKSTAR**

I know, but I've got a plan which is to kill his wife and marry him. When the sun rises, I'll be at the door, then I'll sneak into the sewage system of No 10 Frowning Street and wait for my enemy to approach, then "Boo!", I'll stab her with my sword.

Taseen Khan

## SHUT

But this plan might go wrong because you might attack the wrong person.

## WACKSTAR

Don't put bad luck on me by saying bad things, or I'll stab you with my sword in a minute. Now, because of what you said I'm going to need a second man to help me.

## SHUT

Are you thinking of me being your second man, 'cause it's never gonna happen.

*(WACKSTAR gets out her sword)*

I'll do it

## WACKSTAR

So … the new plan is that you come in the sewage system with me, then make the prime minister's wife fall, and then I'll kill her. And if you make me become the prime minister's wife, I'll make you appear in the Cockroach Apollo show alongside Monskoze, the cockroach comedian.

Taseen Khan

**SHUT**
Who's Monskoze? Is he a good comedian? Is he
as good as Michael McIntyre?

**WACKSTAR**
He's a very good comedian. He's better.

**SHUT**
Fair enough, so long as you don't attack me.
(*Spits on his hand*) Spit promise?

**WACKSTAR**
Yeah, I promise. But I'm never gonna touch your
spit, you filthy banana peel.

**SHUT**
Are we gonna do this now, or are we gonna do it
later?

**WACKSTAR**
Let's call my worm-horse.

**[BLACKOUT]**

Taseen Khan

# SCENE TWO

## TIME
Sunrise. The next day.

## PLACE
No 10 Frowning Street, in the sewage system.

## AT RISE
SHUT and WACKSTAR are trying to climb into the sewage system.

## WACKSTAR
Come on, banana. Stop slipping. Get in!

## SHUT
I've never had a true friend like you.

## WACKSTAR
Come on, I don't have all day, banana.

## SHUT
My name's not banana, it's Shut. That's short for Shut-Hunter-Ulah-Tickletown.

Taseen Khan

## WACKSTAR

My name's Wackstar. Now, let's hurry up, and let's kill the prime minister's wife.

## SHUT

Okay, let me trip her in the bathroom.

*(SHUT goes and lies on the floor. WALKSTAR holds her sword in the air. The COCKRAOCH PRIME MINISTER bursts in)*

## WACKSTAR

Come on. I don't have all day, banana.

## P.M.

Why are you sleeping on my bathroom floor?

## SHUT

I'm not sleeping. I'm just waiting for you to slip over me.

## WACKSTAR

Shut! You just gave the whole thing away! And why does the prime minster's wife sound a bit like a man?

Taseen Khan

## P.M.

It's me, the new prime minister. The old prime mMinister's wife retired because of his age.

## WACKSTAR

Shut! Let me hide behind you!

## P.M.

Don't even think about it! *(Turns the light on)* You're that rubbish highwaywoman who threw a sock at me.

## WACKSTAR

No, I'm not a rubbish highwaywoman. Just listen to how I say the world's most famous words a highwayman-slash-woman could ever say: "Find and kill-over, your trolley or your knife!"

*(Pause. SFX of wind)*

## SHUT

Isn't it meant to be: "Stand and deliver, your money or your life"?

## P.M.

Taseen Khan

She never gets anything right! I've got an important meeting to go to. *(Starts to exit)* *(To SHUT)* Now I'm gonna make sure no cockroach ever helps you.

*(Exit COCKROACH PRIME MINISTER)*

## SHUT
I can't believe I trusted you! I can't believe I thought you were scary, you nincompoop! And what happened to your sword?

## WACKSTAR
Well, when I went to the shops, I got ripped off. The sword was two hundred and fifty-one pounds and fifty-nine pence, but when I went on the bus, it broke.

## SHUT
You're so stupid! Your cockroach brain must be the size of an apple seed.

## WACKSTAR
And what about your comedy life? Don't you need my help? Look, I've got a funny joke. Knock knock.

Taseen Khan

**SHUT**
Who's there?

**WACKSTAR**
Doctor.

**SHUT**
Doctor Who?

**WACKSTAR**
You already said it. (*Drum roll*)

**SHUT**
(*SHUT looks at her. Rolls his eyes and shakes his head*)

Not funny. I'd rather have a five-legged snail help me than you. Now because of you I've got even less chance of becoming a comedian, because even cockroaches won't help me. Thanks a lot, loser!

(*Exit SHUT*)

**WACKSTAR**

Taseen Khan

Why? *(Starts to exit)*
This is the moment when you're supposed to feel
sorry for me and say "aaah".

*(Exit WACKSTAR)*
**[BLACKOUT]**

From a cockroach Prime Minister living at
number '10 Frowning street' to stories
addressing class, poverty and integration in
Camden this book is an intelligent, imaginative
and always funny collection of stories by a
very talented young writer. It's a window onto
the world from an incredibly lively 10 year old
mind that is guaranteed to leave you smiling.
A must read for anyone who wants to see
children's voices taken more seriously and I'm
sure the start of a long career for a budding
talent from Somers Town, Camden.

*Cllr Georgia Gould, Camden Children's
Champion*

Taseen Khan

# Play 3

## The Tour De France Gets Bombed.

### By Taseen Khan aged 12 and Patrick Driver

Time: 2pm
Place: A warzone in Paris, France
At Rise: Jack and Rory are hiding behind blown-up cars.


Jack Jaffa:
Well, this is odd. (Brave)

Rory:
What is? (Petrified)

Jack:
All this.

Rory:
Yes, you could say that. (Sarcastic)

Jack:
Duck! (Noise of bombs) Man I hate this war!

Taseen Khan

Flashback ...

Jack:
I wonder where they're taking them jaffa cakes (looking closer) Oh! It says Buckingham Palace on the label. (Jumps in and gets imported to Buckingham Palace)

Jack:
This is so cool! This palace kitchen is way bigger than Denmark! I love this place!!!

Rory:
(Enters) Shabadingyah! Who are you?

Jack:
No, who are you?

Rory:
Well since you asked, my name is Rory and I am a dirty plate full of curry. I'm 865.3 years old and am an unemployed plate. My dad is breadcrumbs, my mum is a butter dish lid, my brother is a full nice loaf of sliced white bread. 100% satisfaction guaranteed. And my, my sister (cries) she left me, her names Lauren Ralph and –
Jack:

Taseen Khan

Woah, woah, woah! I only asked who you are!
I'm Jack Jaffa, a Jaffa Cake and I'm a lifeguard.

Rory:
Anyways, my sister, she's the only one who can
get me clean! But she's all the way in France.

Jack:
Why don't you go then?

Rory:
I'm too scared to go on my own.

Jack:
You know what, I'll go with you! Maybe I can go
and win the Tour de France while I'm there. I've
always wanted to do that!

Rory:
All right, let's go!

Jack:
(In France) Oh look, there's the Tour de France
sign-up sheet. What!? The tournament is today
starting ... in 10 minutes!

Taseen Khan

Rory:
Come on! You can use that bike and I'll be on the
back seat and read you the maps.
Go faster! The race finishes in Paris and that's
where my sister is!

Jack:
(More cycling) Look, there's the finish!

Rory:
Look, there's my sister. Stop!

Jack:
But I have to win the race!

Rory:
Please, do it for me.

Jack:
No.

Rory :
Yes.

Jack:
No.

Taseen Khan

Rory:
Yes.

Jack:
No, this is my once in a life time opportunity. I MUST WIN!!

Rory:
But there is always next year! Plus if you help me get my sister, I promise you next year that I'll get you the world's fastest bike.

Jack:
(Sighs) Oh all right - stop crying for goodness' sake. (They stop)

A massive bomb explodes

Rory:
Oh no! It's a terrorist attack (They hide)

Jack:
Well this is odd.

Rory:
What is?

Taseen Khan

Jack:
All this.

Rory:
Yes, you could say that. (Sarcastic)

Jack:
Are you okay?

Rory:
Yeah I think so.

Jack:
Look, you promised to help me. Hopefully your sister is all right. So I will help you find her again.

Rory:
Well, sometimes you don't always get what you want...

THE END

Taseen Khan

And cut. Thank you everyone for completing my book. I hope you enjoyed it. I promised you I'd meet you again at the end, didn't I? I always keep my promises. See, I feel like an angel now. Anyways, stay tuned for more of my books. Hope you enjoyed it.

TASEEN KHAN ………...

"Imagination and creativity are the two great driving forces behind our society.
Taseen should be proud of what he has achieved, albeit just the first step in a budding literary career.
*Robert Latham*
*Barrister and Local Resident.*

Taseen Khan